Henri, le Chat Noir

Henri, le Chat Noir

The Existential Musings of an Angst-Filled Cat

WILLIAM BRADEN

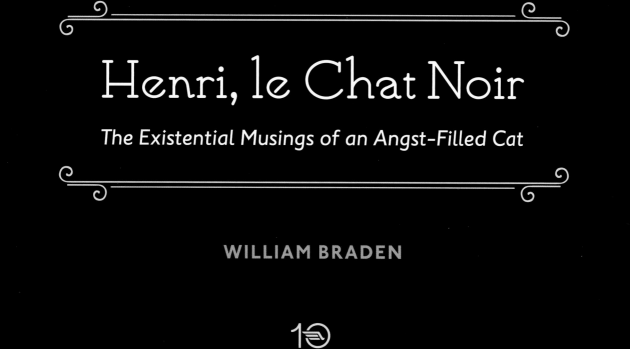

Any cat who searches in vain for truth will experience a profound sense of ennui. I have found that the doors at the end of even the most promising pathways never have cat doors. Alas, I am surrounded by simpleminded cats who do not share my passion for philosophy and my well-meaning but oblivious human caretakers who seem more concerned with a mess on the carpet than philosophy.

Recently, the thieving filmmaker has captured my malaise on film and shared it with the world. Now, I am finally able to put forward my unedited thoughts without his interference. Though my search for answers has, thus far, been fruitless, perhaps somehow I will provide you with new insight. If not, at least this will make you look smart if you leave it on your coffee table.

~ Henri, le Chat Noir

Generally speaking, I do not trust the outside world.

Sartre wrote, "All human actions are equivalent, and all are on principle doomed to failure."

—

This is an eerily prescient commentary on the tardiness of my breakfast.

When I watch you go about your activities, make no mistake about my intentions. I am not curious or coy.

—

I am judging you.

I sleep because every time I open my eyes,
the world is still there.

I rarely purr. Why signal that I am content?

—

I want you to believe that I cannot be mollified,
so you continue your attempts to appease me.

Is there a space between being and nothingness?
Somewhere we drift without relative position or direction?
—

Or is that the catnip talking?

I am a master of camouflage,
and yet I care not whether I am seen.

I watch cats tapping at toys, chasing them around
as though they were real.
—
There is no limit to our delusion.

We cannot escape ourselves.

The white imbecile proves that vacant minds
sleep the most soundly.

Ultimately, our lives are spent diverting ourselves with one meaningless task after another. And yet, the great mysteries of the universe remain undiscovered.

So, does it really matter if I peed on the counter?

Looking into the garden today, I saw another version of myself meeting my gaze. A celestial counterpart, free in all the ways I am trapped, yet longing for the safety of my prison.

—

It turns out it was just a raccoon.

If I am referred to as a deep thinker, it is only because the majority of cats are barely concerned with thought at all.

My thumbs are not opposable, yet I oppose everything.

Inside the box, comfort is implicit yet ephemeral.

Outside the box, comfort is elusive yet permanent.

—

My attempts to combine the two have not met with much success.

Cats, rejoice when your toy rolls under the refrigerator.
You have been freed from jingling plastic subjugation.

The food dish does not know whether it is full or empty.
It simply exists, feeling nothing.

—

I can relate.

They curse the fur on the bed, but what is shedding
if not a reminder of my own spiritual evanescence?
—

It is my soul they vacuum up.

The phone rings, interrupting my slumber. Mysteriously, the phone is knocked from its perch and falls, silenced. Who can say what transpired?

—

Now I sleep, undisturbed by ringing or remorse.

Sir Isaac Newton wrote, "Truth is ever to be found in simplicity, and not in the multiplicity and confusion of things."

—

So, no, you should not consider getting a dog.

I suspect that the various flavors
of my food are really all the same.
Have I convinced myself that variety exists?

—

Even my taste buds deceive me.

Cat treats are a poor substitute for real answers to the mysteries of our existence.

—

Yet, I do not reject them.

I am provided with a superfluous scratching post, although the furniture works just fine.

—

It is foolish to value possessions at the expense of spiritual examination. Each rip of the sofa's fabric is a profound philosophical lesson.

In ancient Egypt, injuring a cat, even accidentally, was punishable by death.

—

Technically, these laws have never been repealed.

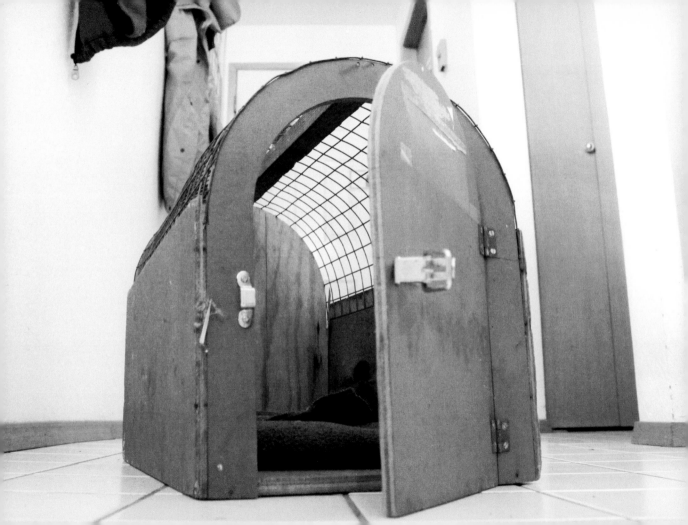

Our choices are not our own.

"Integrity has no need of rules," according to Camus. Therefore, a philosopher cat should be allowed on the counter if he desires. Shooing me away reveals your selfish attempt to keep all the turkey for yourself.

I neither control my tail
nor fully understand its machinations.

—

Do not assume that a playful tail
indicates a playful cat.

As a kitten, I was filled with boundless wonder and an endless need to know more about the world.

I soon discovered the true nature of our existence, and saw it for the cruel and arbitrary prison it is.
Also, I grew into my ears.

Lao-Tzu wrote, "Practice not-doing, and everything will fall into place."

—

Unfortunately, I often find the white imbecile in my not-doing spot.

A man throws a stick, and a dog brings it back
in an endless, slobbery loop.

—

I would leave the stick where it lands, as a reminder
of the transitory nature of our being.

Far removed from his robust and fearless ancestors, the coddled white imbecile cannot brave the snow for more than a few minutes.

—

He is also scared of squirrels.

I have the constant, inescapable burden of seeing
the world as it truly is: meaningless and arbitrary.

—

Why should I care if there are leaves stuck in my fur?

It is difficult to be impressed with any species that submerges itself in water to get clean.

People often wonder if cats climb up to high places
so they can feel superior.

—

This is absurd. Elevation does not affect our superiority.

Even in my own home, I am not immune to barbarity. Who would think it polite to simply throw away the rodent gift I left in the hallway?

—

Humanity, I fear, has lost its way.

During a trip to the vet, I attempted to ask the
doctor about my worsening depressive state.
But he just checked for gunk in my ears.

I often stop and ask myself, "Is this it? Is this all there is?"

Every search for truth must begin somewhere.

—

If mine begins on the couch, who are you to judge?

I experienced fleeting happiness when I heard a can being opened well before dinner time, but it was full of some monstrosity known as "pineapple."

—

Now my despair is all the more piercing, having tasted false hope.

I am surrounded by morons.

My wavering belief in nihilism is affirmed each time the sunbeam moves just when I have drifted off to sleep.

A vast universe of metaphysical truth lies undiscovered all around us, yet I'm supposed to be placated by chasing a little bit of string?

—

My spiritual cup is not so easily filled.

"Distrust everyone in whom the impulse to punish is powerful."
— Nietzsche

Though sitting in the box brings a momentary feeling of contentment, it is, in the end, an illusion.

—

My ennui cannot be contained.

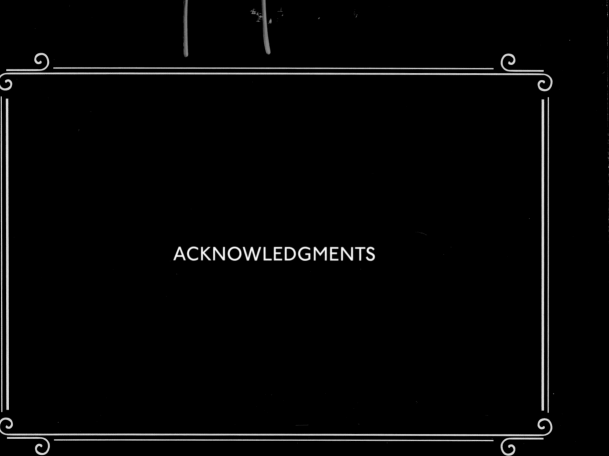

ACKNOWLEDGMENTS

Thank you to Mom, Dad, Kris, and Anna for your endless support and faith, even when I may have been less than deserving of it. Thank you to Katie, Scott, and everyone at the Walker Art Center in Minneapolis for taking cat videos to another level. Thank you to my editor, Melissa, without whose initiative this book would not exist, and without whose expertise it would not be very good at all. Thank you to Betsy for the great design work. Thank you to the thousands of Henri devotees out there around the world. This has been a surreal journey, and it's gratifying to know that so many of you get a chuckle out of Henri's exploits.

And last but not least, thank you to Henry. You may have no idea how famous and beloved the character you portray has become, but were it not for your easygoing personality, I'd never have felt okay with doing any of this. I have to admit that a big part of this whole journey came about just because I like hanging out with you. Enjoy the Party Mix, brother.

Text and photography copyright © 2013 by
William Braden

All rights reserved.
Published in the United States by Ten Speed
Press, an imprint of the Crown Publishing Group,
a division of Random House, Inc., New York.
www.crownpublishing.com
www.tenspeed.com

Ten Speed Press and the Ten Speed Press
colophon are registered trademarks of
Random House, Inc.

Library of Congress Cataloging-in-Publication
Data is on file with the publisher

Hardcover ISBN: 978-1-60774-510-5
eBook ISBN: 978-1-60774-511-2

Printed in China

Design by Betsy Stromberg

10 9 8 7 6 5 4 3 2 1

First Edition